E V I D E N C E

OTHER BOOKS BY MARY OLIVER

POETRY
No Voyage and Other Poems
The River Styx, Ohio, and Other Poems
Twelve Moons
American Primitive
Dream Work
House of Light
New and Selected Poems Volume One
White Pine
West Wind
The Leaf and the Cloud
What Do We Know
Owls and Other Fantasies
Why I Wake Early
Blue Iris
New and Selected Poems Volume Two
Thirst
Red Bird
The Truro Bear and Other Adventures

CHAPBOOKS AND SPECIAL EDITIONS
The Night Traveler
Sleeping in the Forest
Provincetown
Wild Geese (UK Edition)

PROSE
A Poetry Handbook
Blue Pastures
Rules for the Dance
Winter Hours
Long Life
Our World (with photographs by Molly Malone Cook)

EVIDENCE

Poems by

Mary Oliver

BEACON PRESS

BOSTON

Beacon Press
25 Beacon Street
Boston, Massachusetts 02108-2892
www.beacon.org

Beacon Press books
are published under the auspices of
the Unitarian Universalist Association of Congregations.

14 13 12 11 10   8 7 6 5 4 3 2 1

This book is printed on acid-free paper that meets the
uncoated paper ANSI/NISO specifications for permanence
as revised in 1992.

Library of Congress Cataloging-in-Publication Data

Oliver, Mary
Evidence : poems / by Mary Oliver.
p. cm.
ISBN-13: 978-0-8070-6905-9 (alk. paper)
ISBN-10: 0-8070-6905-1 (alk. paper)
I. Title.

PS3565.L5E95 2009
811'.54—dc22
2008036532

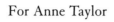

For Anne Taylor

CONTENTS

Yellow 1

Swans 2

Heart Poem 4

Prince Buzzard 5

Li Po and the Moon 7

Thinking of Swirler 8

Snowy Egret 10

Violets 11

Then Bluebird Sang 12

We Shake with Joy 13

Spring 14

The Poet Always Carries a Notebook 16

More Honey Locust 17

Halleluiah 19

It Was Early 20

Water 22

If You Say It Right, It Helps the Heart to Bear It 23

Empty Branch in the Orchard 25

A Lesson from James Wright 27

Deep Summer 28

Almost a Conversation 30

There Are a Lot of Mockingbirds in This Book   31

Prayer   33

At the Pond   34

To Begin With, the Sweet Grass   36

With Thanks to the Field Sparrow, Whose
    Voice Is So Delicate and Humble   40

Landscape in Winter   41

I Want to Write Something So Simply   42

Evidence   43

I Am Standing   47

Schubert   48

Moon and Water   49

When I Was Young and Poor   50

At the River Clarion   51

Philip's Birthday   55

I Want   56

About Angels and About Trees   57

Meeting Wolf   59

Just Rain   60

Mysteries, Yes   62

Imagine   63

First Days in San Miguel de Allende   64

The Trees   68

Broken, Unbroken   69

The Singular and Cheerful Life   71

Another Summer Begins   73

We create ourselves by our choices.
—Kierkegaard

EVIDENCE

Yellow

There is the heaven we enter
through institutional grace
and there are the yellow finches bathing and singing
in the lowly puddle.

Swans

They appeared
  over the dunes,
    they skimmed the trees
    and hurried on

to the sea
  or some lonely pond
    or wherever it is
      that swans go,

urgent, immaculate,
  the heat of their eyes
    staring down
      and then away,

the thick spans
  of their wings
    as bright as snow,
      their shoulder-power

echoing
  inside my own body.
    How could I help but adore them?
    How could I help but wish

that one of them might drop
  a white feather
    that I should have
      something in my hand

to tell me
    that they were real?
      Of course
        this was foolish.

What we love, shapely and pure,
    is not to be held,
      but to be believed in.
        And then they vanished, into the unreachable distance.

Heart Poem

My heart, that used to pump along so pleasantly, has come now to a different sort of music.

There is someone inside those red walls, irritated and even, occasionally, irrational.

Years ago I was part of an orchestra; our conductor was a wild man. He was forever rapping the music-stand for silence. Then he would call out some correction and we would begin again.

Now again it is the wild man.

I remember the music shattering, and our desperate attentiveness.

Once he flung the baton over our heads and into the midst of the players. It flew over the violins and landed next to a bass fiddle. It flopped to the floor. What silence! Then someone picked it up and it was passed forward back to him. He rapped the stand and raised his arms. Then we all breathed again, and the music restarted.

Prince Buzzard

Prince Buzzard,
  I took you, so high in the air,
    for a narrow boat and two black sails.
    You were drifting

in the depths of the air
  wherever you wanted to go,
    and when you came down
      with your spoony mouth

and your red head
  and your creaking wings
    to the lamb
      dead, dead, dead

in the fields of spring
  I knew it was hunger
    that brought you—
      yet you went about it

so slowly,
  settling with hunched wings
    and silent
      as the grass itself

over the lamb's white body—
  it seemed
    a ceremony,
      a pause

as though something
   in the quick of your own body
      had come out
         to give thanks

for the dark work
   that was yours,
      which wasn't to be done easily or quickly,
         but thoroughly—

and indeed by time summer
   opened its green harbors
      the field was nothing but flowers, flowers, flowers,
         from shore to shore

Li Po and the Moon

There is the story of the old Chinese poet:
at night in his boat he went drinking and dreaming
  and singing

then drowned as he reached for the moon's reflection.
Well, probably each of us, at some time, has been
  as desperate.

Not the moon, though.

Thinking of Swirler

One day I went out
  into a wonderful
    ongoing afternoon,
      it was fall,

the pine trees were brushing themselves
  against the sky
    as though they were painting it,
      and Swirler,

who was alive then,
  was walking slowly
    through the green bog,
      his neck

as thick as an ox,
  his antlers
    brushing against the trees,
      his three good feet tapping

the softness beneath him
  and the fourth, from an old wound,
    swirling.
      I know he saw me

for he gave me a long look
  which was as precious as a few
    good words,
      since his eyes

were without terror.
  What do the creatures know?
    What in this world can we be certain about?
    How did he know I was nothing

but a harmless mumbler of words,
  some of which would be about him
    and this wind-whipped day?
      In a week he would be dead,

arrowed down by a young man I like,
  though with some difficulty.
    In my house there are a hundred half-done poems.
      Each of us leaves an unfinished life.

Snowy Egret

A late summer night and the snowy egret
has come again to the shallows in front of my house

as he has for forty years.
Don't think he is a casual part of my life,

that white stroke in the dark.

Violets

Down by the rumbling creek and the tall trees—
   where I went truant from school three days a week
    and therefore broke the record—
there were violets as easy in their lives
   as anything you have ever seen
    or leaned down to intake the sweet breath of.
Later, when the necessary houses were built
   they were gone, and who would give significance
    to their absence.
Oh, violets, you did signify, and what shall take
   your place?

Then Bluebird Sang

Bluebird
   slipped a little tremble
     out of the triangle
      of his mouth

and it hung in the air
   until it reached my ear
     like a froth or a frill
      that Schumann

might have written in a dream.
   Dear morning
     you come
      with so many angels of mercy

so wondrously disguised
   in feathers, in leaves,
     in the tongues of stones,
      in the restless waters,

in the creep and the click
   and the rustle
     that greet me wherever I go
      with their joyful cry: I'm still here, alive!

We Shake with Joy

We shake with joy, we shake with grief.
What a time they have, these two
housed as they are in the same body.

Spring

Faith
is the instructor.
We need no other.

Guess what I am,
he says in his
incomparably lovely

young-man voice.
Because I love the world
I think of grass,

I think of leaves
and the bold sun,
I think of the rushes

in the black marshes
just coming back
from under the pure white

and now finally melting
stubs of snow.
Whatever we know or don't know

leads us to say:
Teacher, what do you mean?
But faith is still there, and silent.

Then he who owns
the incomparable voice
suddenly flows upward

and out of the room
and I follow,
obedient and happy.

Of course I am thinking
the Lord was once young
and will never in fact be old.

And who else could this be, who goes off
down the green path,
carrying his sandals, and singing?

The Poet Always Carries a Notebook

What is he scribbling on the page?
Is there snow in it, or fire?

Is it the beginning of a poem?
Is it a love note?

More Honey Locust

Any day now
the branches
of the honey locust
will be filled
with white fountains;
in my hands
I will see
the holy seeds
and a sweetness
will rise up
from those petal-bundles
so heavy
I must close my eyes
to take it in,
to bear
such generosity.
I hope that you too
know the honey locust,
the fragrance
of those fountains;
and I hope that you too will pause
to admire the slender trunk,
the leaves, the holy seeds,
the ground they grow from
year after year
with striving and patience;
and I hope that you too
will say a word of thanks

for such creation
out of the wholesome earth,
which would be, and dearly is it needed,
a prayer for all of us.

Halleluiah

Everyone should be born into this world happy
  and loving everything.
But in truth it rarely works that way.
For myself, I have spent my life clamoring toward it.
Halleluiah, anyway I'm not where I started!

And have you too been trudging like that, sometimes
  almost forgetting how wondrous the world is
    and how miraculously kind some people can be?
And have you too decided that probably nothing important
  is ever easy?
Not, say, for the first sixty years.

Halleluiah, I'm sixty now, and even a little more,
and some days I feel I have wings.

It Was Early

It was early,
   which has always been my hour
      to begin looking
         at the world

and of course,
   even in the darkness,
      to begin
         listening into it,

especially
   under the pines
      where the owl lives
         and sometimes calls out

as I walk by,
   as he did
      on this morning.
         So many gifts!

What do they mean?
   In the marshes
      where the pink light
         was just arriving

the mink
   with his bristle tail
      was stalking
         the soft-eared mice,

and in the pines
  the cones were heavy,
    each one
      ordained to open.

Sometimes I need
  only to stand
    wherever I am
      to be blessed.

Little mink, let me watch you.
  Little mice, run and run.
    Dear pine cone, let me hold you
      as you open.

Water

What is the vitality and necessity
   of clean water?
Ask the man who is ill, who is lifting
   his lips to the cup.

Ask the forest.

If You Say It Right, It Helps the Heart
to Bear It

The comforts
of language
are true
and deep;

in a cemetery,
in the South,
so many stones
and so many

so small.
Sometimes
three or four
in a row.

In this instance:
Eliza May,
Oceola,
Joseph.

Can you imagine
the condition
of the heart
of a mother

or a father
  watching these plantings?
    I cannot.
      But I try.

"God taketh
  his young lambs home"
    is carved there.
      A few words

like water
  on a stone.
    Cool and beautiful
      like water on a stone.

Empty Branch in the Orchard

To have loved
is everything.
I loved, once,

a hummingbird
who came every afternoon—
the freedom-loving male—

who flew by himself
to sample
the sweets of the garden,

to sit
on a high, leafless branch
with his red throat gleaming.

And then, he came no more.
And I'm still waiting for him,
ten years later,

to come back,
and he will, or he will not.
There is a certain commitment

that each of us is given,
that has to do
with another world,

if there is one.
I remember you, hummingbird.
I think of you every day

even as I am still here,
soaked in color, waiting
year after honey-rich year.

A Lesson from James Wright

If James Wright
could put in his book of poems
a blank page

dedicated to "the Horse David
Who Ate One of My Poems," I am ready
to follow him along

the sweet path he cut
through the dryness
and suggest that you sit now

very quietly
in some lovely wild place, and listen
to the silence.

And I say that this, too,
is a poem.

Deep Summer

The mockingbird
opens his throat
among the thorns
for his own reasons

but doesn't mind
if we pause
to listen
and learn something

for ourselves;
he doesn't stop,
he nods
his gray head

with the frightfully bright eyes,
he flirts
his supple tail,
he says:

listen, if you would listen.
There's no end
to good talk,
to passion songs,

to the melodies
that say
this branch,
this tree is mine,

to the wholesome
happiness
of being alive
on a patch

of this green earth
in the deep
pleasures of summer.
What a bird!

Your clocks, he says plainly,
which are always ticking,
do not have to be listened to.
The spirit of his every word.

Almost a Conversation

I have not really, not yet, talked with otter
   about his life.

He has so many teeth, he has trouble
   with vowels.

Wherefore our understanding
   is all body expression—

he swims like the sleekest fish,
he dives and exhales and lifts a trail of bubbles.
Little by little he trusts my eyes
and my curious body sitting on the shore.

Sometimes he comes close.
I admire his whiskers
and his dark fur which I would rather die than wear.

He has no words, still what he tells about his life
   is clear.
He does not own a computer.
He imagines the river will last forever.
He does not envy the dry house I live in.
He does not wonder who or what it is that I worship.
He wonders, morning after morning, that the river
is so cold and fresh and alive, and still
I don't jump in.

There Are a Lot of Mockingbirds in This Book

Yes, there are many
  of those wondrous creatures
    who live in the thorns
      and are musical all day

and the Lord knows
  when they sleep, for they sing
    in the dark as well,
      as they stare at the moon,

as they flutter a little
  into the air
    then back to the branch,
      back to the thorns—

but this isn't nature
  in which such birds
    want, each pair,
      their own few acres—

this isn't nature
  where the sweetest things,
    being hidden in leaves
      and thorn-thick bushes

reveal themselves rarely—
  this is a book
    of the heart's rapture,
      of hearing and praising

and never forgetting
　　so that the world
　　　　is what the world is
　　　　　in a long lifetime:

singer after singer
　　bursts from the thorn bush,
　　　　now, and again, and again,
　　　　　their songs in the mind forever.

Prayer

May I never not be frisky,
May I never not be risqué.

May my ashes, when you have them, friend,
and give them to the ocean,

leap in the froth of the waves,
still loving movement,

still ready, beyond all else,
to dance for the world.

At the Pond

One summer
  I went every morning
    to the edge of a pond where
      a huddle of just-hatched geese

would paddle to me
  and clamber
    up the marshy slope
      and over my body,

peeping and staring—
  such sweetness every day
    which the grown ones watched,
      for whatever reason,

serenely.
  Not there, however, but here
    is where the story begins.
      Nature has many mysteries,

some of them severe.
  Five of the young geese grew
    heavy of chest and
      bold of wing

while the sixth waited and waited
  in its gauze-feathers, its body
    that would not grow.
      And then it was fall.

And this is what I think
    everything is about:
        the way
            I was glad

for those five and two
    that flew away,
        and the way I hold in my heart the wingless one
            that had to stay.

To Begin With, the Sweet Grass

1.

Will the hungry ox stand in the field and not eat
   of the sweet grass?
Will the owl bite off its own wings?
Will the lark forget to lift its body in the air or
   forget to sing?
Will the rivers run upstream?

Behold, I say—behold
the reliability and the finery and the teachings
   of this gritty earth gift.

2.

Eat bread and understand comfort.
Drink water, and understand delight.
Visit the garden where the scarlet trumpets
   are opening their bodies for the hummingbirds
who are drinking the sweetness, who are
   thrillingly gluttonous.

For one thing leads to another.
Soon you will notice how stones shine underfoot.
Eventually tides will be the only calendar you believe in.

And someone's face, whom you love, will be as a star
both intimate and ultimate,
and you will be both heart-shaken and respectful.

And you will hear the air itself, like a beloved, whisper:
oh, let me, for a while longer, enter the two
beautiful bodies of your lungs.

3.

The witchery of living
is my whole conversation
with you, my darlings.
All I can tell you is what I know.

Look, and look again.
This world is not just a little thrill for the eyes.

It's more than bones.
It's more than the delicate wrist with its personal pulse.
It's more than the beating of the single heart.
It's praising.
It's giving until the giving feels like receiving.
You have a life—just imagine that!
You have this day, and maybe another, and maybe
  still another.

4.

Someday I am going to ask my friend Paulus,
the dancer, the potter,
to make me a begging bowl
which I believe
my soul needs.

And if I come to you,
to the door of your comfortable house
with unwashed clothes and unclean fingernails,
will you put something into it?

I would like to take this chance.
I would like to give you this chance.

5.

We do one thing or another; we stay the same, or we
   change.
Congratulations, if
   you have changed.

6.

Let me ask you this.
Do you also think that beauty exists for some
   fabulous reason?

And, if you have not been enchanted by this adventure—
   your life—
what would do for you?

7.

What I loved in the beginning, I think, was mostly myself.
Never mind that I had to, since somebody had to.
That was many years ago.
Since then I have gone out from my confinements,
   though with difficulty.

I mean the ones that thought to rule my heart.
I cast them out, I put them on the mush pile.
They will be nourishment somehow (everything is nourishment
somehow or another).

And I have become the child of the clouds, and of hope.
I have become the friend of the enemy, whoever that is.
I have become older and, cherishing what I have learned,
I have become younger.

And what do I risk to tell you this, which is all I know?
Love yourself. Then forget it. Then, love the world.

With Thanks to the Field Sparrow, Whose Voice
Is So Delicate and Humble

I do not live happily or comfortably
with the cleverness of our times.
The talk is all about computers,
the news is all about bombs and blood.
This morning, in the fresh field,
I came upon a hidden nest.
It held four warm, speckled eggs.
I touched them.
Then went away softly,
having felt something more wonderful
than all the electricity of New York City.

Landscape in Winter

Upon the snow that says nothing,
that is endlessly brilliant,
there is something
heaped, dark and motionless.

Then come the many wings, strong and bold.
"Death has happened," shout the carrion crows.
"And this is good for us."

I Want to Write Something So Simply

I want to write something
so simply
about love
or about pain
that even
as you are reading
you feel it
and as you read
you keep feeling it
and though it be my story
it will be common,
though it be singular
it will be known to you
so that by the end
you will think—
no, you will realize—
that it was all the while
yourself arranging the words,
that it was all the time
words that you yourself,
out of your own heart
had been saying.

Evidence

1.

Where do I live? If I had no address, as many people
do not, I could nevertheless say that I lived in the
same town as the lilies of the field, and the still
waters.

Spring, and all through the neighborhood now there are
strong men tending flowers.

Beauty without purpose is beauty without virtue. But
all beautiful things, inherently, have this function—
to excite the viewers toward sublime thought. Glory
to the world, that good teacher.

Among the swans there is none called the least, or
the greatest.

I believe in kindness. Also in mischief. Also in
singing, especially when singing is not necessarily
prescribed.

As for the body, it is solid and strong and curious
and full of detail; it wants to polish itself; it
wants to love another body; it is the only vessel in
the world that can hold, in a mix of power and
sweetness: words, song, gesture, passion, ideas,
ingenuity, devotion, merriment, vanity, and virtue.

Keep some room in your heart for the unimaginable.

2.

There are many ways to perish, or to flourish.

How old pain, for example, can stall us at the
threshold of function.

Memory: a golden bowl, or a basement without light.

For which reason the nightmare comes with its
painful story and says: *you need to know this.*

Some memories I would give anything to forget.
Others I would not give up upon the point of
death, they are the bright hawks of my life.

Still, friends, consider stone, that is without
the fret of gravity, and water that is without
anxiety.

And the pine trees that never forget their
recipe for renewal.

And the female wood duck who is looking this way
and that way for her children. And the snapping
turtle who is looking this way and that way also.
This is the world.

And consider, always, every day, the determination
of the grass to grow despite the unending obstacles.

3.

I ask you again: if you have not been enchanted by
this adventure—your life—what would do for
you?

And, where are you, with your ears bagged down
as if with packets of sand? Listen. We all
have much more listening to do. Tear the sand
away. And listen. The river is singing.

What blackboard could ever be invented that
could hold all the zeros of eternity?

Let me put it this way—if you disdain the
cobbler may I assume you walk barefoot?

Last week I met the so-called deranged man
who lives in the woods. He was walking with
great care, so as not to step on any small,
living thing.

For myself, I have walked in these woods for
more than forty years, and I am the only
thing, it seems, that is about to be used up.
Or, to be less extravagant, will, in the
foreseeable future, be used up.

First, though, I want to step out into some
fresh morning and look around and hear myself
crying out: "The house of money is falling!
The house of money is falling! The weeds are
rising! The weeds are rising!"

I Am Standing

I am standing
on the dunes
in the heat of summer
and I am listening

to mockingbird again
who is tonguing
his embellishments
and, in the distance,

the shy
weed loving sparrow
who has but one
soft song

which he sings
again and again
and something
somewhere inside

my own unmusical self
begins humming:
thanks for the beauty of the world.
Thanks for my life.

Schubert

He takes such small steps
to express our longings.
Thank you, Schubert.

How many hours
do I sit here
aching to do

what I do not do
when, suddenly,
he throws a single note

higher than the others
so that I feel
the green field of hope,

and then, descending,
all this world's sorrow,
so deadly, so beautiful.

Moon and Water

I wake and spend
the last hours
of darkness
with no one

but the moon.
She listens
to my complaints
like the good

companion she is
and comforts me surely
with her light.
But she, like everyone,

has her own life.
So finally I understand
that she has turned away,
is no longer listening.

She wants me
to refold myself
into my own life.
And, bending close,

as we all dream of doing,
she rows with her white arms
through the dark water
which she adores.

When I Was Young and Poor

When I was young and poor,
when little was much,
when I was nimble and never tired,
and the hours of the day were deep and long,
where was the end that was already committed?
Where was the flesh that thinned and stiffened?
Nowhere, nowhere!
Just the gift of forgetfulness gracious and kind
while I ran up hills and drank the wind—
time out of mind.

At the River Clarion

1.

I don't know who God is exactly.
But I'll tell you this.
I was sitting in the river named Clarion, on a
   water splashed stone
and all afternoon I listened to the voices
   of the river talking.
Whenever the water struck the stone it had
   something to say,
and the water itself, and even the mosses trailing
   under the water.
And slowly, very slowly, it became clear to me
   what they were saying.
Said the river: I am part of holiness.
And I too, said the stone. And I too, whispered
   the moss beneath the water.

I'd been to the river before, a few times.
Don't blame the river that nothing happened quickly.
You don't hear such voices in an hour or a day.
You don't hear them at all if selfhood has stuffed your ears.
And it's difficult to hear anything anyway, through
   all the traffic, and ambition.

2.

If God exists he isn't just butter and good luck.
He's also the tick that killed my wonderful dog Luke.
Said the river: imagine everything you can imagine, then
   keep on going.

Imagine how the lily (who may also be a part of God)
    would sing to you if it could sing, if
        you would pause to hear it.
And how are you so certain anyway that it doesn't sing?

If God exists he isn't just churches and mathematics.
He's the forest, He's the desert.
He's the ice caps, that are dying.
He's the ghetto and the Museum of Fine Arts.

He's van Gogh and Allen Ginsberg and Robert
Motherwell.
He's the many desperate hands, cleaning and preparing
    their weapons.
He's every one of us, potentially.
The leaf of grass, the genius, the politician,
    the poet.
And if this is true, isn't it something very important?

Yes, it could be that I am a tiny piece of God, and
    each of you too, or at least
        of his intention and his hope.
Which is a delight beyond measure.
I don't know how you get to suspect such an idea.
    I only know that the river kept singing.
It wasn't a persuasion, it was all the river's own
    constant joy
which was better by far than a lecture, which was
    comfortable, exciting, unforgettable.

3.

Of course for each of us, there is the daily life.
Let us live it, gesture by gesture.
When we cut the ripe melon, should we not give it thanks?
And should we not thank the knife also?
We do not live in a simple world.

4.

There was someone I loved who grew old and ill.
One by one I watched the fires go out.
There was nothing I could do

except to remember
that we receive
then we give back.

5.

My dog Luke lies in a grave in the forest,
   she is given back.
But the river Clarion still flows
   from wherever it comes from
     to where it has been told to go.
I pray for the desperate earth.
I pray for the desperate world.
I do the little each person can do, it isn't much.
Sometimes the river murmurs, sometimes it raves.

6.

Along its shores were, may I say, very intense
   cardinal flowers.
And trees, and birds that have wings to uphold them,
   for heaven's sakes—
the lucky ones: they have such deep natures,
   they are so happily obedient.
While I sit here in a house filled with books,
   ideas, doubts, hesitations.

7.

And still, pressed deep into my mind, the river
   keeps coming, touching me, passing by on its
      long journey, its pale, infallible voice
         singing.

Philip's Birthday

I gave,
to a friend that I care for deeply,
something that I loved.
It was only a small

extremely shapely bone
that came from the ear
of a whale.
It hurt a little

to give it away.
The next morning
I went out, as usual,
at sunrise,

and there, in the harbor,
was a swan.
I don't know
what he or she was doing there,

but the beauty of it
was gift.
Do you see what I mean?
You give, and you are given.

I Want

I want to be
in partnership
with the universe

like the tiger lily
poking up
its gorgeous head

among the so-called
useless weeds
in the uncultivated fields

that still abide.
But it's okay
if, after all,

I'm not a lily,
but only grass
in a clutch of curly grass

waving in the wind,
staring sunward: one of those
sweet, abrasive blades.

About Angels and About Trees

Where do angels
  fly in the firmament,
and how many can dance
  on the head of a pin?

Well, I don't care
  about that pin dance,
what I know is that
  they rest, sometimes,
in the tops of the trees

and you can see them,
  or almost see them,
or, anyway, think: what a
  wonderful idea.

I have lost as you and
  others have possibly lost a
beloved one,
  and wonder, where are they now?

The trees, anyway, are
  miraculous, full of
angels (ideas); even
  empty they are a
good place to look, to put
  the heart at rest—all those
leaves breathing the air, so

peaceful and diligent, and certainly
    ready to be
the resting place of
    strange, winged creatures
that we, in this world, have loved.

Meeting Wolf

There are no words
inside his mouth,
inside his golden eyes.

So we stand, silent,
both of us tense
under the speechless but faithful trees.

And this is what I think:
I have given him
intrusion.

He has given me
a glimpse into a better but now broken world.
Not his doing, but ours.

Just Rain

The clouds
did not say
soon, but who can tell
for sure, it wasn't

the first time I had been
fooled; the sky-doors
opened and
the rain began

to fall upon all of us: the
grass, the leaves,
my face, my shoulders
and the flowered body

of the pond where
it made its soft
unnotational
music on the pond's

springy surface, and then
the birds joined in and I too
felt called toward such
throat praise. Well,

the whole afternoon went on
that way until I thought
I could feel
the almost born things

in the earth rejoicing. As for myself,
I just kept walking, thinking:
once more I am grateful
to be present.

Mysteries, Yes

Truly, we live with mysteries too marvelous
  to be understood.

How grass can be nourishing in the
  mouths of the lambs.
How rivers and stones are forever
  in allegiance with gravity
    while we ourselves dream of rising.
How two hands touch and the bonds will
  never be broken.
How people come, from delight or the
  scars of damage,
to the comfort of a poem.

Let me keep my distance, always, from those
  who think they have the answers.

Let me keep company always with those who say
  "Look!" and laugh in astonishment,
  and bow their heads.

Imagine

I don't care for adjectives, yet the world
   fills me with them.
And even beyond what I see, I imagine more.

Seeing, for example, with understanding,
   or with acceptance and humility and
     without understanding,
into the heart of the bristly, locked-in worm
   just as it's becoming what we call the luna,
     that green tissue-winged, strange, graceful,
      fluttering thing.

Will death allow such transportation of the eye?
   Will we see then into the breaking open
     of the kernel of corn,
the sprout plunging upward through damp clod
   and into the sun?

Well, we will all find out, each of us.
   And what would we be, beyond the yardstick,
beyond supper and dollars,
   if we were not filled with such wondering?

First Days in San Miguel de Allende

1.

The flagellated Christ
is being carried
to San Miguel de Allende.
He must be very heavy

yet the carriers persist
upon the sun flashed road
and the people follow

in the same way that people would seek
a river heard of but never yet found.
They are that thirsty.

2.

In the garden the jacaranda
  is dropping
    its blue festivities
      everywhere,

the wren
  is carrying sticks
    into the hollow
      behind the elbow

of the metal horse
  that stands
    in the bougainvillea
      at the edge

of the singing pool.
  I have come, for the first time, to Mexico.
    And what has happened
      to that intense ambition

with which I always wake?
  Soaked up
    in the colors, stolen
      by the bloody Christs

of the churches,
   by the children laughing
      at my meager Spanish.
         It is said

that when you rent a house here
   the owners are not responsible
      for church bells, barking dogs,
         or firecrackers.

It is early in the morning.
   Antonio is sweeping the blossoms away.
      I am feeling something, incredibly,
         like peace.

The wren is busy, my pencil idle.
   The silks of the jacaranda, as though
      it is the most important work in the world,
         keep falling.

3.

The tops of the northbound trains are dangerous.
Still, they are heaped with hopefuls.

I understand their necessity.
Understanding, however, is not sharing.

Oh, let there be a wedding of the
   mind and the heart, if not today
      then soon.

Meanwhile, let me change my own life
   into something better.

Meanwhile, on the streets of San Miguel de Allende
   it is easy to smile.
"Hola," I say to the children.
"Hi," they say, as I pass

with my passport, and money, in my pocket.

The Trees

Do you think of them as decoration?

Think again.

Here are maples, flashing.
And here are the oaks, holding on all winter
    to their dry leaves.
And here are the pines, that will never fail,
    until death, the instruction to be green.
And here are the willows, the first
    to pronounce a new year.

May I invite you to revise your thoughts about them?
Oh, Lord, how we are all for invention and
    advancement!
But I think
    it would do us good if we would think about
these brothers and sisters, quietly and deeply.

The trees, the trees, just holding on
    to the old, holy ways.

Broken, Unbroken

The lonely
stand in the dark corners
of their hearts.

I have seen them
in cities,
and in my own neighborhood,

nor could I touch them
with the magic
that they crave

to be unbroken.
Then, I myself,
lonely,

said hello to
good fortune.
Someone

came along
and lingered
and little by little

became everything
that makes the difference.
Oh, I wish such good luck

to everyone.
How beautiful it is
to be unbroken.

The Singular and Cheerful Life

The singular and cheerful life
of any flower
in anyone's garden
or any still unowned field—

if there are any—
catches me
by the heart,
by its color,

by its obedience
to the holiest of laws:
be alive
until you are not.

Ragweed,
pale violet bull thistle,
morning glories curling
through the field corn;

and those princes of everything green—
the grasses
of which there are truly
an uncountable company,

each
on its singular stem
striving
to rise and ripen.

What, in the earth world,
is there not to be amazed by
and to be steadied by
and to cherish?

Oh, my dear heart,
my own dear heart,
full of hesitations,
questions, choice of directions,

look at the world.
Behold the morning glory,
the meanest flower, the ragweed, the thistle.
Look at the grass.

Another Summer Begins

Summer begins again.
How many
do I still have?
Not a worthy question,

I imagine.
Hope is one thing,
gratitude another
and sufficient

unto itself.
The white blossoms of the shad
have opened
because it is their time

to open,
the mockingbird
is raving
in the thornbush.

How did it come to be
that I am no longer young
and the world
that keeps time

in its own way
has just been born?
I don't have the answers
and anyway I have become suspicious

of such questions,
and as for hope,
that tender advisement,
even that

I'm going to leave behind.
I'm just going to put on
my jacket, my boots,
I'm just going to go out

to sleep
all this night
in some unnamed, flowered corner
of the pasture.

I thank the editors of the following magazines in which some of the poems have previously appeared, sometimes in slightly different form.

Five Points: "Heart Poem"
Michigan Quarterly: "Swans"
Onearth: "Violets"
Orion: "At the Pond"
Parabola: "Li Po and the Moon," "Snowy Egret," "Water"
Portland Magazine: "Just Rain"
Shenandoah: "Thinking of Swirler," "Halleluiah," "It Was Early,"
  "If You Say It Right, It Helps the Heart to Bear It"
Southern Review: "Prince Buzzard," "To Begin With, the Sweet Grass"
Spiritus: "Spring"